CREATIVE AMERICA

PUBLISHED FOR THE NATIONAL CULTURAL CENTER BY THE RIDGE PRESS

EDITOR IN CHIEF AND PUBLISHER: Jerry Mason

ART DIRECTOR: Albert A. Squillace

PROJECT EDITOR: Thomas B. Morgan

EDITOR: Adolph Suehsdorf

ASSOCIATE PROJECT EDITOR: Michael Mason

ASSOCIATE EDITOR: Evelyn Hannon

ASSOCIATE ART DIRECTOR: Leon Bolognese

ART CO-ORDINATOR: Doris Mullane

FOR MAGNUM: Lee Jones, Sam Holmes

PRODUCTION: Allied Graphic Arts

EDITORIAL ADVISORY COMMITTEE

K. LeMoyne Billings

Norman Cousins

John Fischer

Frank Gibney

Hiram Haydn

William D. Patterson

Joseph J. Thorndike, Jr.

Cover photo by Wayne Miller

© 1962 by THE RIDGE PRESS, INC.

551 Fifth Avenue, New York, New York

Library of Congress Catalog Card Number 62-21401

Robert Frost poem, page 62

copyright © 1962 by Robert Frost.

Reprinted by permission of Holt, Rinehart and Winston, Inc.

Printed in the United States of America

This book has been created for the National Cultural Center. The national center for the performing arts is about to be built in Washington. Creative America is conceived in its spirit. It is a book about creation in all the arts. It is not a survey or an encyclopedia. But it is an attempt to picture the circle of creation: It starts with the sources of inspiration. It shows work beginning—the first struggle with an idea and the attempt to put it on paper, or on canvas, or in stone, or on stage. Elation is there as the work advances. So is dejection. There is the finished work—and its audience. The circle continues as learning begins and youth reaches out for new aspirations. The circle comes full. When man creates, he is affirming his individuality and his humanity. This book, like the National Cultural Center, is dedicated to that spirit.

CONTENTS

¶ One afternoon in the fateful year 1941, the President of the United States had two callers. The first was Lord Lothian, the British Ambassador, who had just flown in from London to give Franklin D. Roosevelt an eyewitness account of the bombing of London. The second was Francis H. Taylor, museum director and authority on the history of art.   ¶   Taylor waited for two hours while the President and Lothian talked. When he finally entered, he found the President "white as a sheet." Yet the President, we are told, kept Taylor in his office that afternoon for another hour and a half. Turning from a grim preoccupation with the war, Franklin Roosevelt talked about the arts in American life. He spoke of plans for broadening the appreciation of art, and looked forward to a day when "every schoolhouse would have contemporary American paintings hanging on its walls."   ¶   George Biddle, the distinguished American artist who records this meeting, adds on his own: "Roosevelt had little discrimination in his taste in painting and sculpture. [But] he had a more clear understanding of what art could mean in the life of a community—for the soul of a nation—than any man I have known."   ¶   In the same year of 1941, Roosevelt himself recalled another President who also found time in the midst of great national trials to concern himself with artistic endeavors. It was in the third year of the Civil War—as Roosevelt told the story in a speech dedicating the National Gallery in Washington, D.C.—and men and women had gathered to see the Capitol dome completed and the bronze goddess of liberty set upon the top. "It had been an expensive and laborious business," Roosevelt said, "diverting labor and money from the prosecution of the war, and certain critics . . . found much to criticize. There were new marble pillars in the Senate wing of the Capitol; there was a bronze door for the central portion and other such expenditures and embellishments. But the President of the United States—whose name was Lincoln—when he heard these criticisms, answered: 'If the people see the Capitol going on, it is a sign that we intend this Union shall go on.'"   ¶   Both Roosevelt and Lincoln understood that the life of the arts, far from being an interruption, a distraction, in the life of a nation, is very close to the center of a nation's purpose—and is a test of the quality of a nation's civilization. That is why we should be glad today that the interest of the American people in the arts seems at a new high.

THE ARTS IN AMERICA *by John F. Kennedy*

❡ Looking at the American scene, I am impressed by its diversity and vitality—by the myriad ways in which Americans find enlightenment, exercise, entertainment, and fulfillment. Everyone, young and old, seems to be busy. Our roads and seashores are crowded; the great parks draw visitors in unprecedented numbers. Sports thrive, and even such formerly humdrum activities as buying groceries for the family take on a holiday aspect in the new shopping centers. In the midst of all this activity, it is only natural that people should be more active in pursuit of the arts. ❡ The statistics are gratifying—books have become a billion-dollar business; more money is spent each year in going to concerts than to baseball games; our galleries and museums are crowded; community theaters and community symphony orchestras have spread across the land; there are an estimated thirty-three million Americans who play musical instruments. And all this expresses, I believe, something more than merely the avidity with which goods of all kinds are being acquired in our exuberant society. A need within contemporary civilization, a hunger for certain values and satisfactions, appears to be urging us all to explore and appreciate areas of life which in the past we have sometimes neglected in the United States. ❡ Too often in the past, we have thought of the artist as an idler and dilettante and of the lover of arts as somehow sissy or effete. We have done both an injustice. The life of the artist is, in relation to his work, stern and lonely. He has labored hard, often amid deprivation, to perfect his skill. He has turned aside from quick success in order to strip his vision of everything secondary or cheapening. His working life is marked by intense application and intense discipline. As for the lover of arts, it is he who, by subjecting himself to the sometimes disturbing experience of art, sustains the artist—and seeks only the reward that his life will, in consequence, be the more fully lived. ❡ Today we recognize increasingly the essentiality of artistic achievement. This is part, I think, of a nationwide movement toward excellence—a movement which had its start in the admiration of expertness and skill in our technical society, but which now demands quality in all realms of human achievement. It is part, too, of a feeling that art is the great unifying and humanizing experience. We know that science, for example, is indispensable—but we also know that science, if divorced from a knowledge of man and of man's ways, can stunt a civilization. And so the educated man—and very often the man who has had the best scientific education—reaches out for the experience which the arts alone provide. He wants to explore the side of life which expresses the emotions and embodies values and ideals of beauty.

¶ Above all, we are coming to understand that the arts incarnate the creativity of a free society. We know that a totalitarian society can promote the arts in its own way—that it can arrange for splendid productions of opera and ballet, as it can arrange for the restoration of ancient and historic buildings. But art means more than the resuscitation of the past: it means the free and unconfined search for new ways of expressing the experience of the present and the vision of the future. When the creative impulse cannot flourish freely, when it cannot freely select its methods and objects, when it is deprived of spontaneity, then society severs the root of art. ¶ Yet this fact surely imposes an obligation on those who acclaim the freedom of their own society—an obligation to accord the arts attention and respect and status, so that what freedom makes possible, a free society will make necessary. ¶ I have called for a higher degree of physical fitness in our nation. It is only natural that I should call, as well, for the kind of intellectual and spiritual fitness which underlies the flowering of the arts.

¶ A nation's government can expect to play only an indirect and marginal role in the arts. Government's essential job—the organization and administration of great affairs—is too gross and unwieldy for the management of individual genius. But this does not mean that government is not, or should not be, concerned with the arts. A free government is the reflection of a people's will and desire—and ultimately of their taste. It is also, at its best, a leading force, an example, and teacher. I would like to see everything government does in the course of its activities marked by high quality. I would like to see the works of government represent the best our artists, designers, and builders can achieve. I want to make sure that policies of government do not indirectly or unnecessarily put barriers in the way of the full expression of America's creative genius. ¶ The arts in the United States are, like so many other of our activities, varied and decentralized to a high degree. Private benefactors, foundations, schools and colleges, business corporations, the local community, the city, and the state, combine in widely differing proportions to organize and support the institutions of culture. I would hope that in the years ahead, as our cultural life develops and takes on new forms, the Federal government would be prepared to play its proper role in encouraging cultural activities throughout the nation. ¶ In the nation's capital, the Federal government, of course, has special obligations. There is, first, the fact that the District of Columbia lies directly within Federal jurisdiction. Beyond this, there is the fact that, as the capital of our nation, Washington inevitably becomes to a degree a showcase of our culture. In other countries, capitals have been located in great cities with an historic identity and cultural life of their own. But Washington, it has been remarked, is a single-industry town—and that industry is politics and statecraft. Such an environment, some have said, provides barren soil for the arts. Yet, despite this, the community of Washington has done much to welcome and encourage cultural activity. ¶ Still, our vision must look beyond the pleasure of the community to the leadership of the nation. In this vision, the National Cultural Center will play a vital role. The Center, which Congress has chartered and for which it has given land, aims to be part of a broad effort to stimulate the performing arts. It was not conceived as a group of halls and theaters to benefit Washington audiences alone. Here visitors and tourists will come throughout the year, bringing back to their communities a sense of what the performance of great works can mean in their lives—and a proud realization that their nation's capital is a focus of creative activities. In many other ways, the National Cultural Center will interact with the cultural life of communities across the country. The finest of our symphony orchestras will play here; local repertory theaters and opera and ballet groups, increasing in numbers and professional status, should find their appearance in the nation's capital a distinction eagerly sought. The Center will, I hope, become in the broadest sense an educational as well as a cultural institution, helping to stimulate the formation of similar groups in other cities. ¶ Other countries have their national theater and opera, permanently situated in the capital and singled out for their government's special concern. Better fitted to the needs of the United States is the idea of the Cultural Center, a great stage hospitable to the best coming from this country and abroad, an institution encouraging the development of the performing arts in all their diversity of origin and variety of form. I earnestly hope that the backing of citizens across the country will make possible the fulfillment of these plans.

¶ To work for the progress of the arts in America is exciting and fruitful because what we are dealing with touches virtually all the citizens. ¶ There will always be of necessity, in any society, a mere handful of genuinely creative individuals, the men and women who shape in words or images the enduring work of art. Among us, even this group tends to be enlarged. "I hear America singing," said Walt Whitman. He would certainly hear it singing with many voices if he were alive today. ¶ Outside the group of active participants stands the great audience. Perhaps no country has ever had so many people so eager to share a delight in the arts. Individuals of all trades and professions, of all ages, in all parts of the country, wait for the curtain to rise—wait for the door that leads to new enjoyments to open. ¶ This wonderful equality in the cultural world is an old American phenomenon. Tocqueville, in the 1830's, described how on the remotest frontier, in a wilderness that seemed "the asylum of all miseries," Americans preserved an interest in cultural and intellectual matters. "You penetrate paths scarcely cleared," said Tocqueville, "you perceive, finally, a cleared field, a cabin . . . with a tiny window." You might think, he continues, that you have come at last to the home of an American peasant. But you would be wrong. "The man wears the same clothes as you; he speaks the language of the cities. On his rude table are books and newspapers." ¶ The cabin with its tiny window has vanished. Yet we might expect to find its counterparts today in homes which would seem quite as remote from the arts. The suburban housewife harassed by the care of her children, the husband weary after the day's work, young people bent on a good time—these might not appear in a mood to enjoy intellectual or artistic pursuit. Still on the table lie paper-bound reprints of the best books of the ages. By the phonograph is a shelf of recordings of the classics of music. On the wall hang reproductions of the masterpieces of art. ¶ To further the appreciation of culture among all the people, to increase respect for the creative individual, to widen participation by all the processes and fulfillments of art—this is one of the fascinating challenges of these days.

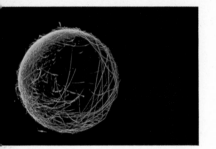  

NEW JERSEY . ERNST HAAS

KANSAS . ERICH HARTMANN

MAINE . ERNST HAAS

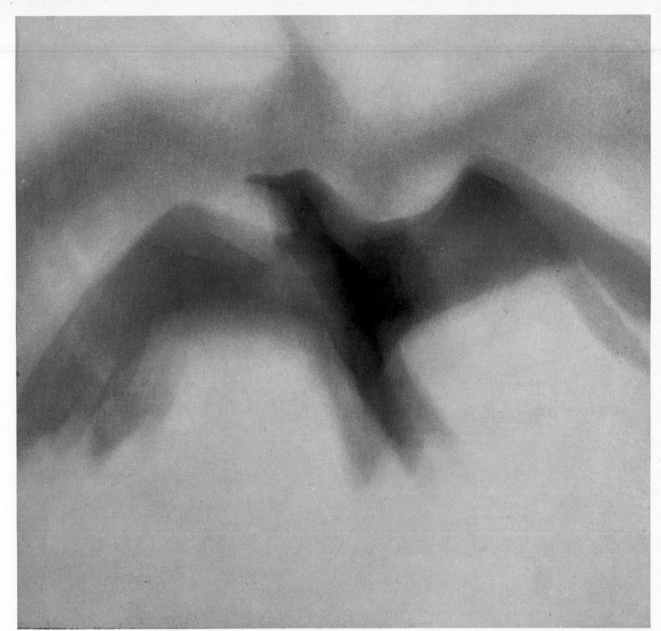

CALIFORNIA . ERNST HAAS

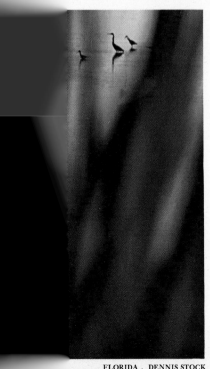

FLORIDA . DENNIS STOCK

NEW YORK . ERNST HAAS

PENNSYLVANIA . ERNST HAAS

UTAH . ERNST HAAS   NEW YORK . DAN BUDNIK

CALIFORNIA . ERNST HAAS

¶ Perhaps the primary distinction of the artist is that he must actively cultivate that state which most men, necessarily, must avoid: the state of being alone. That all men *are*, when the chips are down, alone, is a banality—a banality because it is very frequently stated, but very rarely, on the evidence, believed. Most of us are not compelled to linger with the knowledge of our aloneness, for it is a knowledge which can paralyze all action in this world. There are, forever, swamps to be drained, cities to be created, mines to be exploited, children to be fed: and none of these things can be done alone. But the conquest of the physical world is not man's only duty. He is also enjoined to conquer the great wilderness of himself. The role of the artist, then, precisely, is to illuminate that darkness, blaze roads through that vast forest; so that we will not, in all our doing, lose sight of its purpose, which is, after all, to make the world a more human dwelling place. ¶ The state of being alone is not meant to bring to mind merely a rustic musing beside some silver lake. The aloneness of which I speak is much more like the aloneness of birth or death. It is like the fearful aloneness which one sees in the eyes of someone who is suffering, whom we cannot help. Or it is like the aloneness of love, that force and mystery which so many have extolled and so many have cursed, but which no one has ever understood or ever really been able to control. I put the matter this way, not out of any desire to create pity for the artist— God forbid!—but to suggest how nearly, after all, is his state the state of everyone, and in an attempt to make vivid his endeavor. The states of birth, suffering, love, and death, are extreme states: extreme, universal, and inescapable. We all know this, but we would rather not know it. The artist is present to correct the delusions to which we fall prey in our attempts to avoid this knowledge. ¶ It is for this reason that all societies have battled with that incorrigible disturber of the peace—the artist. I doubt that future societies will get on with him any better. The entire purpose of society is to create a bulwark against the inner and the outer chaos, literally, in

THE CREATIVE PROCESS *by James Baldwin*

order to make life bearable and to keep the human race alive. And it is absolutely inevitable that when a tradition has been evolved, whatever the tradition is, that the people, in general, will suppose it to have existed from before the beginning of time and will be most unwilling and indeed unable to conceive of any changes in it. They do not know how they will live without those traditions which have given them their identity. Their reaction, when it is suggested that they can or that they must, is panic. And we see this panic, I think, everywhere in the world today, from the streets of our own New Orleans to the grisly battleground of Algeria. And a higher level of consciousness among the people is the only hope we have, now or in the future, of minimizing the human damage. ⁋ The artist is distinguished from all the other responsible actors in society—the politicians, legislators, educators, scientists, et cetera—by the fact that he is his own test tube, his own laboratory, working according to very rigorous rules, however unstated these may be, and cannot allow any consideration to supersede his responsibility to reveal all that he can possibly discover concerning the mystery of the human being. Society must accept some things as real; but he must always know that the visible reality hides a deeper one, and that all our action and all our achievement rests on things unseen. A society must assume that it is stable, but the artist must know, and he must let us know, that there is nothing stable under heaven. One cannot possibly build a school, teach a child, or drive a car without taking some things for granted.

The artist cannot and must not take anything for granted, but must drive to the heart of every answer and expose the question the answer hides. ⁋ I seem to be making extremely grandiloquent claims for a breed of men and women historically despised while living and acclaimed when safely dead. But, in a way, the belated honor which all societies tender their artists proves the reality of the point I am trying to make. I am really trying to make clear the nature of the artist's responsibility to his society. The peculiar nature of this responsibility is that he must never cease warring with it, for its sake and for his own. For the truth, in spite of appearances and all our hopes, is that everything is always changing and the measure of our maturity as nations and as men is how well prepared we are to meet these changes and, further, to use them for our health. ⁋ Now, anyone who has ever been compelled to think about it—anyone, for example, who has ever been in love—knows that the one face which one can never see is one's own face. One's lover —or one's brother, or one's enemy—sees the face you wear, and this face can elicit the most extraordinary reactions. We do the things we do, and feel what we feel, essentially because we must—we are responsible for our actions, but we rarely understand them. It goes without saying, I believe, that if we understood ourselves better, we would damage ourselves less. But the barrier between oneself and one's knowledge of oneself is high indeed. There are so many things one would rather not know! We become social creatures because we cannot live any other way. But in order to become social, there are a great many other things which we must not become, and we are frightened, all of us, of those forces within us which perpetually menace our precarious security. Yet, the forces are there, we cannot will them away. All we can do is learn to live with them. And we cannot learn this unless we are willing to tell the truth about ourselves, and the truth about us is always at variance with what we wish to be. The human effort is to bring these two realities into a relationship resembling reconciliation. The human beings whom we respect the most, after all— and sometimes fear the most—are those who are most deeply involved in this delicate and strenuous effort: for they have the unshakable authority which comes only from having looked on and endured and survived the worst. That nation is healthiest which has the least necessity to distrust or ostracize or victimize these people—whom, as I say, we honor, once they are gone, because, somewhere in our hearts, we know that we cannot live without them.   ❡   The dangers of being an American artist are not greater than those of being an artist anywhere else in the world, but they are very particular. These dangers are produced by our history. They rest on the fact that in order to conquer this continent, the particular aloneness of which I speak—the aloneness in which one discovers that life is tragic, and, therefore, *therefore*, unutterably beautiful—could not be permitted. And that this prohibition is typical of all emergent nations will be proven, I have no doubt, in many ways during the next fifty years. This continent now is conquered, but our habits and our fears remain. And, in the same way that to become a social human being one modifies and suppresses and, ultimately, without great courage, lies to oneself about all one's interior, uncharted chaos, so have we, as a nation, modified and suppressed and lied about all the darker forces in our history. We know, in the case of the person, that whoever cannot tell himself the truth about his past is trapped in it, is immobilized in the prison of his undiscovered self. This is also true of nations. We know how a person, in such a paralysis, is unable to assess either his weaknesses or his strengths, and how frequently indeed he mistakes the one for the other. And this, I think, we do. We are the strongest nation in the western world, but this is not for the reasons that we think. It is because we have an opportunity which no other nation has of moving beyond the Old World concepts of race and class and caste, and create, finally, what we must have had in mind when we first began speaking of the New World. But the price for this is a long look backward whence we came and an unflinching assessment of the record. For an artist, the record of that journey is most clearly revealed in the personalities of the people the journey produced. Societies never know it, but the war of an artist with his society is a lover's war, and he does, at his best, what lovers do, which is to reveal the beloved to himself, and with that revelation, make freedom real.

PAINTER WILLEM DE KOONING . DAN BUDNIK

ERNST HAAS

PHOTOGRAPHER EDWARD STEICHEN . WAYNE MILLER

WRITER JAMES BALDWIN . MARC RIBOUD

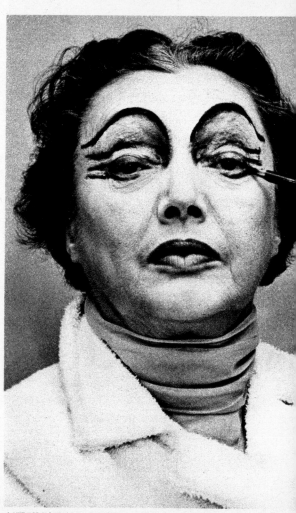

ACTRESS KATHARINE CORNELL . DENNIS STOCK

TEACHER-POET PAUL ENGLE . WAYNE MILLER

ACTRESS ANNE BANCROFT . BRUCE DAVIDSON

POET MARIANNE MOORE . ELLIOTT ERWITT

WRITER JOHN STEINBECK . ERICH HARTMANN

PIANIST RUDOLF SERKIN . ERICH HARTMANN

CHOREOGRAPHER GEORGE BALANCHINE . ERNST HAAS

COMPOSER RICHARD RODGERS . EVE ARNOLD

CONDUCTOR THOMAS SCHIPPERS . CONSTANTINE MANOS

CONDUCTOR ROBERT CRAFT . ERNST HAAS

PHOTOGRAPHER BERT STERN . BRUCE DAVIDSON

COMEDIAN MORT SAHL . HENRI CARTIER-BRESSON

CONDUCTOR LEOPOLD STOKOWSKI . DENNIS STOCK

PAINTER HELEN FRANKENTHALER . BURT GLINN

ACTRESS JULIE HARRIS, ACTOR ROBERT REDFORD . HENRI CARTIER-BRESSON

WRITER ARTHUR MILLER . EVE ARNOLD

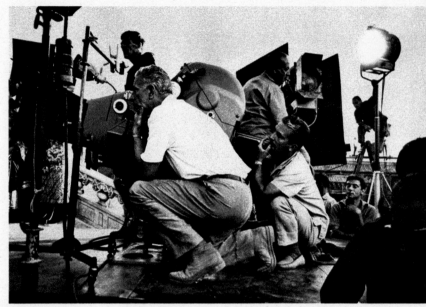

DIRECTOR NICHOLAS RAY . DENNIS STOCK

WRITER HENRY MILLER . MARC RIBOUD

MUSICIANS RED GARLAND, MILES DAVIS . DENNIS STOCK

ACTORS JASON ROBARDS, JR., DEAN STOCKWELL . BOB HENRIQUES

PRODUCER ALEXANDER COHEN, DIRECTOR ARTHUR PENN . DENNIS STOCK

STRUCTURAL DESIGNER BUCKMINSTER FULLER . ELLIOTT ERWITT

ARCHITECT EDGAR TAFEL . DENNIS STOCK

WRITER WILLIAM CARLOS WILLIAMS . EVE ARNOLD

DIRECTOR KIRK BROWNING . ERNST HAAS

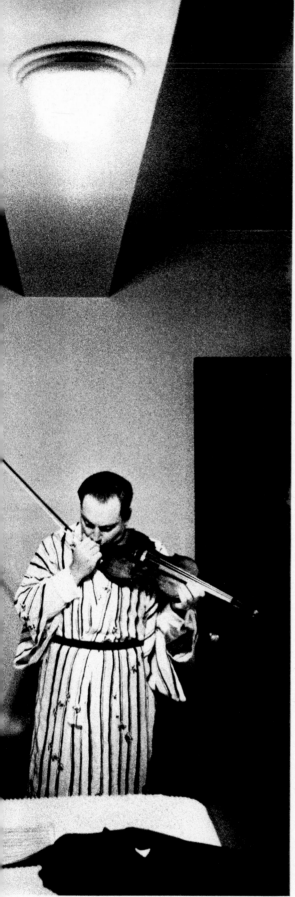

VIOLINIST ISAAC STERN . DENNIS STOCK

POET GREGORY CORSO . BURT GLINN

CARTOONIST SAUL STEINBERG . INGE MORATH

SINGER ETHEL MERMAN . DENNIS STOCK

SOPRANO EILEEN FARRELL . BRUCE DAVIDSON

CONDUCTOR-COMPOSER LEONARD BERNSTEIN . BRUCE DAVIDSON

MUSICIANS ERNIE ROYAL, JIMMY MUNDY, BUCK CLAYTON . DENNIS STOCK

PIANIST RUDOLF SERKIN . BRUCE DAVIDSON

DIRECTOR JOHN HUSTON . ERNST HAAS

MUSICIANS GERRY MULLIGAN, JIMMY GIUFFRE, JIM HALL · DENNIS STOCK

DANCER RUTH SOBOTKA . ERNST HAAS

DIRECTOR JOHN HUSTON . INGE MORATH

BALLET SCORE: IGOR STRAVINSKY . ERNST HAAS

SCULPTOR ERNESTO GONZALEZ . DAN BUDNIK

ACTRESS KATHARINE HEPBURN . DENNIS STOCK

MUSICIAN PUNCH MILLER . DENNIS STOCK

¶ In one sense, the United States has been the most tirelessly "creative" nation in history. No other has been so given to creating new appliances, devising short cuts, contriving fresh angles. Consider our achievements in slang, or in showmanship, or in amusements; think what we have done just to advance the sandwich: club, combination, triple-decker, ice-cream, hero. Think how, since wigwam days, we have varied our habitations, right on to the skyscraping and split level, the trailer home on wheels, the trail blazer's over a waterfall. Dismiss, if you will, a hundred useful thoughts like the bottle cap, there remain the telegraph, the telephone, the electric light. Ignore miniature golf and drive-in movies, poker remains, and baseball and basketball, and jazz. ¶ Along such largely unaesthetic lines, it's all too easy, of course, to say that we have created all too little. Yet, as creatively no nation has shown a more public or social face, none has shown one more private and solitary—Thoreaus and Hawthornes, Emily Dickinsons and Ryders. If we have instituted the public-address system, we have all but perfected the private language; against a Coney Island must be set a Walden Pond; against bumper-to-bumper traffic emerge death on a pale horse, a whaling vessel's crazed captain, a doomed Negro adrift in West Indian waters, an enshuttered spinster in an Amherst house. If we are notorious for our conformists, we have long been proverbial for our cranks; if we everlastingly make pacts with Mammon, we constantly seek peace from God. ¶ Now these extremes are not merely picturesque; they are pointedly instructive. For clearly the one extreme in large measure derives from the other. The nation of P. T. Barnum and publicity bred not just a desire, but a burning need, for privacy. The nation of George F. Babbitt and Rotary begot not just no impulse to join, but a compulsion to turn away. And what this evokes, for me, is a great triptych of America's creative life whose center panel is curiously inadequate and incomplete. The side panels are truly extraordinary, but in the absence of a vibrant living center there has been nothing to bridge the distance between the other two, or keep them—the one so aloof, the other so gregarious—from glaring at each other. ¶ We have

THE CREATIVE ARTS *by Louis Kronenberger*

had, of course, central creative artists of many kinds, whether a Whitman or a Louis Sullivan, a Dreiser or a Robert Frost. But even our *major* creative figures have often not been truly central ones, and our greatest creative need still is to provide a spacious, populous center panel. What America has lacked creatively is an art that is in the most adult sense human, in the most organic sense social; that can be accessible and enriching to a great number of people, yet without watering its meaning or pandering in its appeal. What the Renaissance and Elizabethan England produced in art, architecture, drama, and poetry, or nineteenth-century Europe in fiction, music, opera —this is what one means by central, spacious, permeating. And this is what America has never fully had—not just for possessing no Balzac or Verdi, but no lasting body of social fiction either, no real flowering of opera at all. Functioning too publicly or privately, for too many or too few, our creative activity has oftener suggested schism than coalescence. And all the more because of this, today's great cultural problem, today's great creative predicament, is to achieve for America resonant, unifying voices with no loud-speaker overtones; large, illuminating vistas with no Technicolor trimmings.   ❡   Any such process, any such product, cannot be speeded up—a necessary warning, surely, to a nation with whom speed is an obsession. Nor can it just be blueprinted or built to order: we can be pretty sure that the next Balzac won't very much resemble the last one. The process, in any case, demands as many safeguards as incentives, as much rudder as sail. Talent abounds in this country today; in poetry, for example, or in painting, the roster of names is remarkable. And in this country today, there is not simply a decided recognition of the artist's importance, there is a genuine recognition of his needs. That recognition is nowhere more sharply dramatized than on the present occasion; but it is everywhere evident, in a prodigality of grants and fellowships and awards, in a variety of artists' colonies and academic residencies, in a host of readings and recitals and exhibitions, a heap of commissions to paint or design or compose. And this ever-growing encouragement to create chimes in with an ever-growing interest in the already created, with the great boom in quality paperbacks, art books, and long-playing records. More than that, our creativeness has achieved, if only in minor and popular forms, a kind of leadership, of pace setting for the world. We have led the world in jazz and musical comedy, in mad humor and wild westerns, in certain forms of storytelling, in vivid language now current in fifty tongues, in bright contributions to the art or convenience of living. And all this points up a national gift that makes for a central art—our enormous energy and vitality. ❡ Such manifestations are splendid, and could be greatly enlarged upon. If what I stress instead is safeguards—is stop lights—it is because our pace and energy can make for wrong turns in the road, or short cuts that come out at the wrong place. Thus, we have been creatively most successful where most commercial (musical comedy, industrial design), or most utilitarian (packaging, highway systems). Creatively we have been next most successful where least commercial, as with poetry. Where our success seems disturbingly mixed is in creative forms, such as fiction and the theater, that are equally capable of serious impact or popular appeal. In contemporary fiction we have perhaps had writers of potentially as genuine talent, from Faulkner down, as from Frost down in poetry. And if much gifted novel writing has fallen short, or even fallen apart, it involved work that had to impose form on unruly substance, that had to manage both the quick swoop and the sustained flight, that had to throw light and perspective on today's confused and confusing world. Any failure to do this was wholly forgivable; what seems much less so is how often the creative process turned flabby or factitious or shallow, showed loud-speaker overtones or Technicolor trimmings, or seemed seduced by a rather too worldly prestige. Hence—whether or not we rather glibly call the result middle-brow—there was a weakening of fiber, a blurring of edges, in too many novels; a botching and surrendering of values in too many plays. In the established theater, seriousness, when not bogged down in the clumsy, seems hardly able to keep in motion without the slick. In the theater, at even its most talented, violence or corruption is often handled corruptly. The very producers, again, with the sharpest eye for talent have the surest touch for tarnishing it. And along with its vulgarizing goes the theater's passion for adaptations as against original work—a constant slap at the creative spirit. And if a form of adulteration and commercialism menaces the novel and the stage, another—of faddish and fashionable collecting—has allied painting with the stock market hardly less than with the studio.   ❡   What America has most of all created is fads, few of them good friends to the creative process. They reflect a seeming contradiction in our culture: our need of conformity, yet our craving—but it is a herdlike craving—for novelty. And our enjoyment of what is appealingly novel has increased our dislike of what is disconcertingly, often subversively, new. As a result, we have developed critical zones as extremist as our creative ones: a too-bubbly, easy going, tolerant journalistic criticism; an academic criticism too hidebound, toplofty, excommunicatory. In criticism, too—despite certain redeeming figures, of whom Edmund Wilson stands foremost—the center panel has a sparse look and a squeezed one.   ❡   If I may speak once more of the creative center panel—of the full-bodied art that is its desideratum, and the "middle-brow" pressures that constitute its danger—it is that we just cannot leave the matter to the artist alone, but must bring in the audience as well. Mr. Dore Schary once dubbed us as a "happy-ending nation"; and just so, much gifted center-panel creative work ends in blur and betrayal. Too many Americans will, for example, accept the highly charged, the violent, the vicious, the "ugly" side of life, as a form of excitement, but not of personal involvement, of vital experience. Hence too much that might be consistently creative tends now to be a little softened, now a little sensationalized. The artist's loss of "integrity" in all this can be quite unconscious, a matter indeed of diminished acuteness or awareness. It's all very well, it's even sometimes true, to say that the artist can compel his vision of life upon his age. But, generally speaking, a creativity that is to retain all its independence without becoming crabbedly recusant, or chronically satiric, or increasingly eccentric, or deficient in poise and perspective—a creativity that is to be permeating—needs a porous, responsive culture, a supple and adventurous audience. High-flown, unrealistic notions of the Creative Spirit can be as harmful as Philistine ones.   ❡   What is so appalling in American life—most of Hollywood and TV, many best sellers and box-office hits, treacly music and flashy art—is a wholly different problem, a problem of cultural slum clearance that nowhere affects the creative process. The creative problem lies with the gifted work—fiction, drama, music, art—that slightly mars its gifts: the glasses not rose-colored, only tinted; the truths not violated, merely veiled. Or it lies with the gifted work that stretches and forces its gifts, not through loss of probity from within, but through the pressure of offers or inducements from without. Hurried, half-smudged creative work, born of being too much in demand, can prove as damaging as hack work born of too little. In a happy-ending nation—and let's not fool ourselves, we are often that at quite superior cultural and educational levels—creativity must show twice the firmness and vigilance it might show elsewhere. In a happy-ending nation its function is particularly to expose, discredit, expunge the wishful and the sentimental, the generally accepted and the effortlessly understood. And if in one way or another—it would be invidious to mention names—it does get tired or overextended, does abdicate its proper role, does acquiesce in what it ought to combat, it is not for us to feel guiltless. Talent does not guarantee strong character or unyielding values, and the creativity that for the artist is a personal gift remains for others, for us, a cultural responsibility. ❡ Creatively, almost everything in America points to success except our worship of success; almost everything argues a place in the sun except our craving for the limelight. These aside, the situation is extremely favorable to creative work. "Madison Avenue," for example, could as readily be a symbol today for art galleries as for advertising and TV; our sky lines today could as often be symbols of a dynamic architecture as of an industrial society. As for individual names, any proper list of those boasting creative promise or achievement must run to improper lengths. Even if restricted to the middle generation or younger, the poets, the painters, and not too much less the composers are many—and varied to boot. Even thus restricted, in a field where I have planted a question mark—fiction—there are, for a mere starter, Saul Bellow, Eudora Welty, Bernard Malamud; or among the still very young, Philip Roth or John Updike; or certainly, though fact may be outdistancing fiction, James Baldwin. In the theater, to be sure, any names later than Williams and Miller are no better than promising; but the theater has its gifted interpreters; has the special talents, like those of a Nichols and May; has impressively—whether for his ballets or his staging—a Jerome Robbins. This is indeed an ideal occasion to salute America's abundant creative activity, and to support the creative process—on its own terms, not ours.

VIOLINIST RICHARD WETMORE . BRUCE DAVIDSON

ACTRESSES ANNE BANCROFT, PATTY DUKE . DENNIS STOCK

STONE STEPS

Put stone steps anywhere and time sets in.
Builders make steps climb. Time takes them down.
Look at Rome's warped stones. Every man,
woman, child going up to pray scuffs the stone
one prayer thinner. Before it's gone
workmen come by and lay a new one.
But only a stopgap. Begin again
anywhere; you only begin again. The first foot on
the block is as legal as the last one.
What's done is not done instantly, but it is done.

There gets to be less and less to climb by—to prayer
or to anything. If workmen do not get there
in time you find a ramp instead of a stair.
If no one gets there, you find a mound where
the ramp was and nothing on top. Why are
stones thought to be solids? Air
is as long. It is only faster than they are,
not less firm. Air, moreover, can repair
itself. What stone can? And you can climb higher
on air than on stone. If you are
out for altitude build accordingly. If you dare.

JOHN CIARDI

ENTERTAINER SAMMY DAVIS, JR . BURT GLINN

SOLOMON R. GUGGENHEIM MUSEUM, NEW YORK . DENNIS STOCK

IN A GLASS OF CIDER

It seemed I was a mite of sediment
That waited for the bottom to ferment
So I could catch a bubble in ascent.
I rode up on one till the bubble burst
And when that left me to sink back reversed
I was no worse off than I was at first.
I'd catch another bubble if I waited.
The thing was to get now and then elated.

ROBERT FROST

CONDUCTOR WILLIAM STEINBERG . CONSTANTINE MANOS

NEWPORT JAZZ . ERNST HAAS

TIME & LIFE BUILDING, NEW YORK, ARCHITECTS HARRISON & ABRAMOVITZ & HARRIS . ERNST HAAS

"THE BOOK OF JOB ." DENNIS STOCK

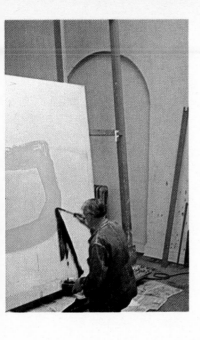

PAINTER WILLEM DE KOONING . DAN BUDNIK

POET ROBERT FROST . BURT GLINN

ACTOR ZERO MOSTEL . DENNIS STOCK

WRITER JOHN UPDIKE . DENNIS STOCK

"CAMELOT." DENNIS STOCK

SCULPTOR LEONARD BASKIN . DENNIS STOCK

ARCHITECT EDWARD BARNES . DENNIS STOCK

PAINTER PAUL RESIKA . ELLIOTT ERWITT

NEW YORK PHILHARMONIC . BRUCE DAVIDSON

SOPRANO ANNA MOFFO . DENNIS STOCK

NEW YORK CITY BALLET . ERNST HAAS

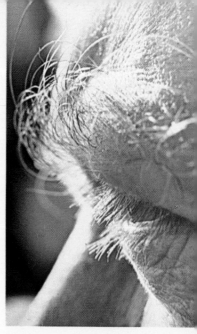
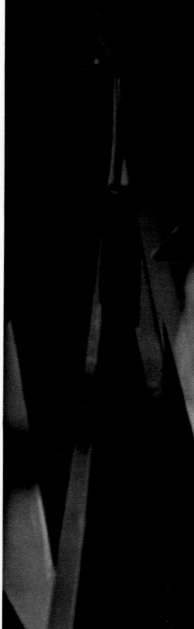

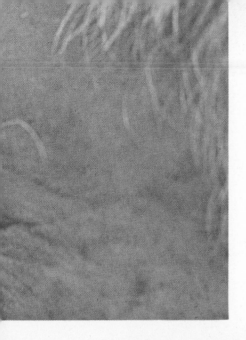

SCULPTOR ALEXANDER CALDER . DENNIS STOCK

FIRST PRESBYTERIAN CHURCH, STAMFORD, CONN., ARCHITECT WALLACE K. HARRISON · ERNST HAAS

AUDIENCE, METROPOLITAN OPERA HOUSE . BRUCE DAVIDSON

MUSEUM OF MODERN ART, NEW YORK . EVE ARNOLD

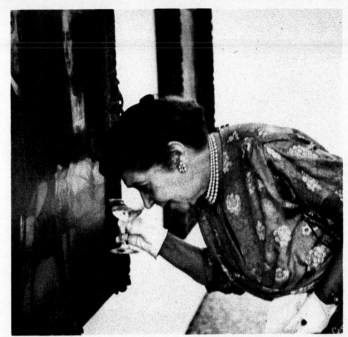

DE YOUNG MUSEUM, SAN FRANCISCO . EVE ARNOLD

MUSEUM OF FINE ARTS, HOUSTON . EVE ARNOLD

COLISEUM, NEW YORK . DAN BUDNIK

SOLOMON R. GUGGENHEIM MUSEUM . DENNIS STOCK

ACADEMY AWARD . DENNIS STOCK

WRITER PAUL GOODMAN . HENRI CARTIER-BRESSON

ACTRESS SUSAN STRASBERG, ACTOR FRANCHOT TONE . DENNIS STOCK

¶ Before the creative spirit can be communicated to the young, or to those of any age who do not have it yet, it must be defined with all possible care, lest it be misunderstood at the very outset. Misunderstanding in this case can be serious; indeed, it can be fatal to the spirit in question. And the commonest form of misunderstanding consists of supposing that man ever does create anything—that is to say, causes it to come into existence, brings it into being, or originates it. Man simply does not have that power, though sometimes he seems to think so. His genius and his glory lie in an altogether different direction: he is an imitator, not a creator. ¶ To call him an imitator may seem to belittle him, but it might be well to consider whether any other creature can do even that. No other creature can. All creatures, including man, find themselves in a world they did not make and could not have made. And man alone is capable of comprehending what this means. He alone can see the world as something outside of himself which he can reflect in that unique mirror, his mind. It is a unique mirror in that it is more than quicksilver and glass. It studies, it penetrates, it sees parts of things in relation to one another; in the scientist it combines and recombines those parts so that something entirely new may seem to result. But it is not entirely new, any more than the so-called creations of the artist are entirely new—made up, so to speak, out of things that had no previous existence. The scientist and the artist are alike in that they begin with existence, and go on from there to imitations or reconstructions of it, which by their brilliance can blind us to the fact that nothing after all has been brought into being. All that has happened is that being itself has become clearer and more beautiful to us than it was before. This is a superb achievement, and it does not belittle man to claim that he is capable of it. Rather do we then perceive his ultimate, his incomparable distinction.   ¶   The

THE CREATIVE HERITAGE *by Mark Van Doren*

greatest artists are the most lifelike: the best imitators of life. Their works, we say, are so much like life that they might be life themselves. But they are not life; they are like life, and it gives us happiness to realize that this is so. If Shakespeare is the best of poets, the reason surely is that he misses less than other poets do of the world he renders. We say he leaves nothing out; he sees everything in its full form and at its right value, and, finally, he causes what he sees, and what he makes us see, to glow with its own natural color. But he does not make us see what was never there. We had seen it too, over and over. The difference now is that we love it more, and behold it with a deeper intelligence. There is nothing new in Shakespeare except this beauty in everything, which he has helped us see more completely than we had considered possible. No man could have done more for other men. ❡ Was Shakespeare, then, "original"? What would it mean to call him so? He has never in fact been paid the compliment, if compliment it is. Nor can he be imagined as ever desiring that it should be paid him. He would rather have been praised as true —true to the life he found himself living with others. He would rather have heard it said of him that he noticed this life in all of its particulars. He was the greatest of noticers. And the child or the youth who has ambitions to be an artist should be asked if *he* is a noticer. What we call creation is nothing but noticing—and then, of course, reflecting and rendering what has been noticed. But first of all, noticed. The artist has good eyes and ears, and uses them as most of us do not. He uses them to observe and relish what is *there,* outside himself or in; for he notices too how his own mind works, and lets none of its operations elude him. Yet his own mind, being the human mind, is like all other minds, just as the world outside of it is the same world for us all. We did not make our minds any more than we made the world they have the gift to mirror. The most original artist knows this the most humbly, and is the most likely to wish that we would judge his works by their truth, comparing it to what we already know. ❡ He is also the most willing that we should compare his account of life with the accounts of other artists. To the extent that he competes with them, he expects to be measured by a standard common to all artists, and this standard is the truth, the whole truth, and nothing but the truth. If originality means trying something that no one ever tried before and no one will ever try again, then comparison ceases to be possible. The good artist prefers to be measured for results that can be stated. He is not, of course, concerned in any of his works with the whole truth at once. Particular truth is his practical aim. And toward this end he has selected a form which he will make as perfect as he can. The best art comes out of many attempts by many artists to write the same poem, paint the same picture, compose the same symphony or song. As soon as this is done perfectly—by Shakespeare, by Congreve, by Mozart, by Rembrandt—the effort moves into another field. But it was a concerted effort on the part of many persons who accepted the same rules. The artist who triumphed was original only in the intensity and the fullness with which he realized the possibilities of the form. The form was before him, as his success will live after him. ❡ A young person who wants to practice a given art should be convinced first that it is indeed an art. It is a way of imitating life, and there are demands which it makes upon anyone who woos it. The chief of these demands are knowledge and love, not only of life itself, but of the means men take to reflect it. The artist loves his art, too, and in his apprentice days learns to love the masters who preceded him in its practice. The artist imitates other artists, and surpasses them if he can. But he begins by trying what they tried, and the better the artists he imitates, the faster he will improve—as Keats did, once he discovered Shakespeare, Milton, and Spenser. Left to himself, Keats might never have been impressive. He might have gone on merely trying to express himself. The proper business of the artist is not to express himself; it is to express the world, and the dimensions of the world are most clearly seen in the works of great artists. We can make them clearer still, but that will be hard work. The good artist will not hesitate to undertake it.   ¶   Nor will he feel that he loses anything by learning. He will understand that the more he knows about life, and about the art he is compelled to practice, the better he will be. Compelled is not too strong a word for the desire that moves him. The good artist is born as well as made: born with the desire to do what we find him doing. But he *must* be made. So he delights to learn. Granted that he might never have written a poem if he had never read one, or painted a picture if he had never seen one—granted this, he now proceeds as if he were free, as in fact he is, to be first in the field if he can. He will never be free to be first, however, unless he understands that he is also last—the last to try what has been tried by a long line of artists before him. He goes to school to his art, and likes it.   ¶   Imitation and learning. We learn about life, and we learn to imitate it. To communicate the importance of these essentials is the best way to inspire a beginning artist. For one thing, it may relieve him of certain terrors, lest creation be the mysterious, the magic process it is all too frequently represented to him as being. The only mysterious matter is that some of us have the desire to be artists and some do not. But given the desire, the next thing to understand is that knowledge plays an indispensable role in the formation of the poet, the painter, the sculptor, the musician. It has been said that the more a lawyer knows about everything, the better a lawyer he will be. And so of doctors, and divines, and statesmen. And precisely the same thing is true of artists. They do not start from scratch; they start by scratching—by peering, by digging, by diving and coming up again. Their art was there before them, just as life was, which they will now set out to render. Nor will they lose by being in a given case just one kind of artist instead of another. Nobody ever felt sorry for Shakespeare because he was nothing but a poet, for Rembrandt because he was nothing but a painter, for Bach because he was nothing but a musician. Each had his own way—but it was the way of others too—of learning all there was for him to learn. Or for him to make us learn. For it is well to remember how much we learn from artists. What we learn is not absolutely new, but we learn it in the most delightful of senses. We recognize it. Which means that we know it again, and better; more deeply, more clearly, more humbly with respect to its power and beauty.

¶ It was said a long time ago that there is nothing new under the sun. It could also have been said—and doubtless it was—that there is nothing newer than this morning's sunrise, or the infant born today. Life, which never changes, is always starting over. And so is any art. The newest poet may be the best. But we shall not say this of him if there is no basis for comparison with others. The basis is his knowledge of the thing he imitates and of the art by which that is to be done. Inspiration is largely emulation of the artists we adore. But first of all, there must be some artists we adore. We must know and love them before we can surpass them. And so with life. We must know and love it before we can imitate its grandeurs.

WAYNE MILLER

BRUCE DAVIDSON

WAYNE MILLER

EVE ARNOLD

WAYNE MILLER

EVE ARNOLD

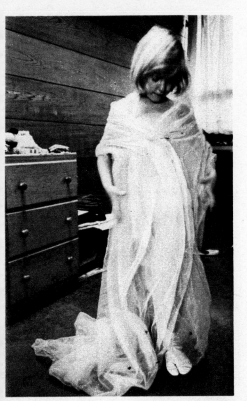

WAYNE MILLER

MUSIC STUDENTS . DENNIS STOCK

TEACHER-ARCHITECT WALTER GROPIUS . BURT GLINN

STUDENT CHORUS . CONSTANTINE MANOS

99

SCULPTURING CLASS . ELLIOTT ERWITT

STUDENT ARCHITECT . BURT GLINN

BALLET CLASS . ERNST HAAS

TEACHER-POET PAUL ENGLE . WAYNE MILLER

PAINTING STUDENT . EVE ARNOLD

DRAMA STUDENTS . BRUCE DAVIDSON

ART STUDENT . BRUCE DAVIDSON

PAINTING STUDENT . ELLIOTT ERWITT

¶ The growing enthusiasm among our people for the arts is an expression of deeply rooted American aspirations—a modern rededication, so to speak, to fundamental American attitudes.

¶ In the earliest beginnings of the Republic, a concern for the arts and the cultural aspects of human living characterized its life. What has survived of that time to this day, from public buildings to the tools of commerce and craft, demonstrates that our ancestors believed utility and beauty were companions. ¶ Moreover, the founding fathers—a group unique in the grandeur and the reach of their political vision—were men acutely aware that a dynamic society cannot rest content with merely material accomplishment. Their dream of a new society in a new world included beauty widely enjoyed as well as wealth widely shared. They dreamed of a nation adept at the arts of humanism as well as at the works of industry. They strove for cultural growth as well as for economic increase. ¶ To be sure, for the superficial observer of later days, the hallmark of the American way became the pace of expansion across the continent, the exploitation of natural resources, technical inventiveness, and the housing and clothing and feeding of a multiplying population. But the dream and the hunger for the realization of beauty in daily life was never lost.

¶ Now, the renewed concern among our people for the arts is a significant development in this era of the Republic's history. It affects directly the quality of our national life. For example: symphony concerts and art museums are prime sources of new inspiration and strength for daily living; books, in their number and variety, beget new perspectives on all facets of human relations

THE CREATIVE PURPOSE *by Dwight D. Eisenhower*

—not excluding politics—creative hobbies foster new satisfaction in personal achievement. ❡ Today, many thousands of Americans are Sunday painters. Many more thousands are avid amateur musicians, sculptors, actors, and craftsmen. The typical American community has its chamber-music group, its poetry society, its little theater, its classes for student artists of all ages. And as these efforts provide rewarding experiences for individuals, still more Americans become aware of the pleasure and profit for good living that await them in the arts. ❡ At the same time, career artists have a new and greater influence in our society. Their genius sets them up as an example for those to whom art is an avocation. Moreover, their access to various media of communication enables them to offer their works to great masses of interested people, and especially the young. Thus, they have today a very special place in our lives and a very special responsibility. They express America's concepts of beauty, decency, and morality. Their talent and their freedom give them an opportunity to help shape their fellow citizens' aesthetic and ethical standards. They can uplift taste or debase it. Theirs, it seems to me, is a vital responsibility because it affects the morale of our country—indeed, it affects our soul. ❡ Artists fully aware of and dedicated to their responsibility strengthen our national spirit. Artists cognizant of their opportunity and willing to seize it contribute to our national aspirations. Their new place in American life should, I think, inspire new and finer accomplishments—in all the arts. It is my hope that they, in turn, will inspire us with new pride in the concepts of mind and heart that have made our country great.

¶ I think that there is general agreement here and abroad that in things material we have made the greatest strides in the history of man and that we have forged ahead in most fields of human endeavor. The question often raised by some of our critics is whether we have not accomplished this unprecedented development at the expense of the aesthetic progress of our society. The answer is clearly in the negative. I believe that our progress in the areas of the arts and culture has been no less dramatic. Indeed, we have wrought better than some thought we had a right to expect when we take into account the huge amounts of energy our people have devoted to building this nation, not only as a "home of the free," but as a place where almost everyone is, or can be, well off. We have, in fact, produced an environment where the material and the cultural are in highly favorable balance. ¶ The artists among us are the men and women who work, think, and dream in their efforts to let us know where we stand in our advancement toward our ideals. It seems to me that we can hardly get along without our artists, as we must also recognize that they cannot get along without us. ¶ Creativity is not a secret force limited

THE CREATIVE PURPOSE *by Harry S. Truman*

only to those people born with artistic talent. The experimenter in the laboratory, the representative of the people in his legislature, the teacher in a classroom are often inspired in ways that can only be called "creative." Yet the artist is the one member of our society whose every effort is totally dependent on creativity. If we value him, we must also value that which enables him to create. I think that creativity grows best where there is freedom of the individual and free government. ❡ There is a new way, a new opportunity for us to begin a new era in the arts. It is not the easy way; it is always easier to vote funds and let the government try to do it. The fact is that more than money and other tangible forms of public support, our artists need a richer soil in which to create. They need to live and work in a community that cherishes freedom of expression. In the regimented society the artist withers. In the intolerant society he is consumed by his antagonisms. In the materialistic society he feels isolated. It seems to me that we serve art best when we serve the ideals of American society. As we expand freedom and resist all attempts to restrict it, we not only benefit ourselves, we also create the ideal conditions for art.

ERNST HAAS

WAYNE MILLER

DENNIS STOCK

115

ERNST HAAS

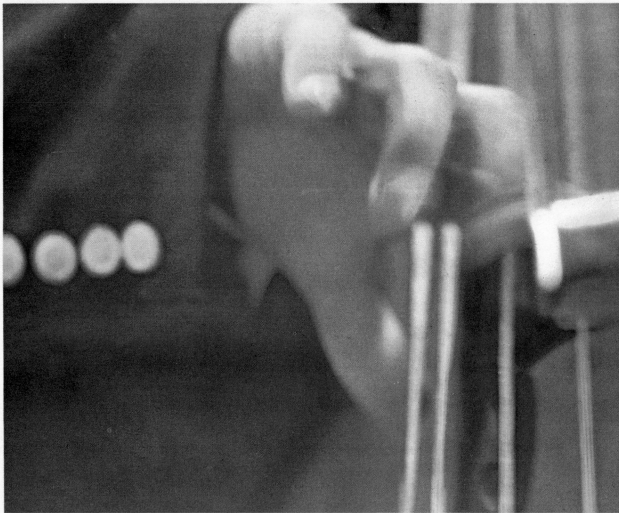

ERNST HAAS

ERNST HAAS

BURT GLINN

¶ The story of man's adventures and achievements on this planet can be told in many different ways. Today it is most often told in terms of his technological advances—which is to say in terms of his assumption of power over his physical environment. Sometimes it is assumed, even, that any other achievements are mere consequences of his success in this grand enterprise, and extremists have gone so far as to suggest that the measure of a civilization is simply the horsepower available per unit of population. Nevertheless, the story can also be told in various other ways such as, for instance, in terms of his beliefs, ideals, convictions, and standards of value. Sometimes, though less often, it has been told in terms of his creative imagination as revealed in his art.   ¶   All of these things go hand in hand. All are manifest in the earliest, or at least almost the earliest, evidence we have of man's existence as an animal who had begun to exhibit characteristics different from those of any other animal. He had hardly invented the first crude tools and weapons before he began to ornament them and, in this as well as in other ways, to exhibit his concern with something other than naked utility. Thus he invented not only art, but also ritual and religion as accompaniments of his various practical techniques, and he became man the thinker and dreamer as soon, or almost as soon, as he became man the maker.   ¶   To be human has always meant to be concerned, to some extent, with a complex of activities which involve both those directed toward survival and physical comfort on the one hand; on the other, those which furnish an occupation for mind and spirit. The impulse to invent or represent through the medium of words or lines is as natural and spontaneous as any other impulse toward the fulfillment of inherent capacities. It manifests itself early in the childhood of the individual and in the childhood of the race. To inhibit or frustrate it is to risk anxiety and discontent.   ¶   Notoriously, however, the development of this or that aspect of man's multiple activities and interests has been most rapid and successful at some times and among some peoples. We speak with admiration of the achievements of this nation or culture as they are evident in science, or art, or philosophy, or government.

CREATIVE AMERICA *by Joseph Wood Krutch*

Sometimes technology stands nearly idle while artistic creation and graceful social customs flourish so astonishingly that a single century transforms almost out of recognition the mental landscape among which a people lives. The Greeks wrote poetry, history, and philosophy by the light of smoky lamps whose design had changed hardly at all in ten thousand years.   ¶   Perhaps the Greeks did not change the lamps they wrote and read by because all their interest and effort was centered upon what they were writing and reading. Perhaps we rushed from a lamp not very much better than theirs to the fluorescent light in approximately one hundred and fifty years, while making no such advances in other desirable directions, because it was just in technology that we discovered our special talents.   ¶   It has been cynically said that whereas the Middle Ages learned how to build cathedrals, it was reserved to us to discover how they could be most quickly and completely destroyed. That is an aspect of the truth which may, indeed, be as important as the other aspect—which is that we have also enormously increased the length, comfort, and at least temporary security of human life. In any case, the central fact is beyond dispute: ours has been an age in which man the maker has triumphed spectacularly, while the creative imagination which produces art—to put it so mildly that the statement can hardly be questioned—has not manifested itself sufficiently for us to outshine and outclass the ages which went before us.   ¶   Those who not only admit but emphasize this fact take various attitudes toward it. The simplest is to say that we should continue to devote our effort and attention to the development of those talents we have discovered to be particularly ours; to leave other enterprises to other peoples and other times. Some have gone even further. They say we have discovered not only the correct enterprise for us, but, after many millennia of fumbling with impossible aims and meaningless questions, what the human being is really fitted for. According to them, Aristotle was guilty of a fundamental mistake when he answered the question, "What is man for?" by replying, "for contemplation." Man, so some of Aristotle's successors insist, is a stupendously clever maker, while his aspirations in other directions are doomed to perpetual frustration. The so-called fine arts, as well as all thought other than scientific description of phenomena and the discovery of the ways in which the physical world may be manipulated, belong to the infancy of the race. The man of the future will lose his taste for them. He will acquire more power, comfort, and security. He will be interested only in utility and function. He will be content to have become exclusively man the maker—and the maker of only those things which directly serve his survival or his comfort. ⸿ Not many have expressed this conviction in so extreme a form or in terms of a logical extraction, but it is related to what was, not unnaturally perhaps, a widely prevalent attitude in a country that was rushing forward as rapidly as ours, from wilderness to its present position as the richest, most powerful, and technologically most advanced nation in the world. ⸿ A late nineteenth-century tycoon is said to have remarked in all simplicity that America had no need of artists, since we were in a position to buy from Europe all the treasures of the past which we had any use for. And though there were only a few who had arrived at a conviction so clear and concise, those who thought (or even did not think at all) on the subject, assumed that artistic creation and artist appreciation were frills—well enough in their way, but best left to elegant, otherwise unemployed women and to those male misfits who were somehow incapable of doing the world's work, while virile and capable men devoted their energies to inventing machines, building factories, and accumulating wealth. If, as the second Samuel Butler said, Englishmen supported the vicars of the Church of England in order to have someone to be virtuous for them vicariously, so even the more enlightened members of the American plutocracy were willing to do no more than give rather contemptuous support to those who would, vicariously, create or admire art for them. ⸿ This assumption that the arts are, but are actually no more than, ornaments and graces superimposed upon the solid structure of a civilization is, of all assumptions, the most stultifying. The most dangerous enemy of intellectuality, as well as of artistic creation, is neither the exponent of science and technology nor, on the other hand, the simple Philistine. The most dangerous enemy is the one who pays lip service to art as somehow desirable enough as long as it is regarded as the mere graceful embellishment of a prosperous life, rather than as an activity which, since the first emergence of man, has been a concern of every fully developed human being. As President George Schuster has so wisely said, a civilizing education cannot aim or wish to produce a nation composed exclusively of saints, philosophers, and artists. But it ought to aim at producing one in which every educated man can to some extent participate in the experience of the saint, the philosopher, and the artist.　❡　To what extent is that ideal being approached in the United States today? On the one hand, there certainly exists a body of writers, painters, and composers larger than ever before; also a larger audience for their work than ever before. What critics call "high art" engages the attention of a considerable public, while "the popular arts" are responsible for an entertainment industry which both creates and absorbs more wealth than any similar enterprise in the whole history of the world.　❡　Yet the situation is not as encouraging as might at first sight seem. Though a considerable number of high-brows and the majority of those content to accept classification in the low-brow category put their faith in movies, television, jazz, and popular music as new forms of a folk art out of which an art great by any standards will grow, there is a fallacy in their argument: most if not all of our popular art is not folk art at all, but something manufactured, handed down, and even imposed upon a sort of captive audience.　❡　The creators of a genuine folk art are themselves members of the folk. They share its interests, tastes, preoccupations, and standards. Like the makers of proverbs, their work represents the wisdom of many and the wit of one. But Hollywood, Madison Avenue, and tin-pan alley are not folk institutions. The most successful creators who operate with them are likely to collect Picassos or read James Joyce. To them their audience is what Hollywood used to call "the peasants." They calculate and contrive what these peasants will like.　❡　As an extreme, but not unrepresentative, example take the case of a very popular TV performer who was interviewed in a recent issue of "TV Guide" (June 9 to 15, 1962) concerning his attitude toward a sensationally successful serial. This performer lives on an estate in the San Fernando Valley. For years he studied music. Classical composition is his favorite pastime. His living room contains a Steinway concert grand and a thirteenth-century tapestry; "The rest of the house abounds in antiques and unusual art objects." Yet concerning his major occupation, the manufacture of a serial which has just been renewed for the fifth year, he has this confession to make: he no longer studies his lines. "I just skim over them before each scene. The dialogue and the character don't change; just the locations." It is a glowing tribute, he says, to the writers that "audiences are able to watch the show without losing their dinners." He would like to depart quickly from the series, but is restrained by a contract. "I have no serious gripe. It's been good to me. But now it becomes a question of which will live longer, the show or me. I'm hoping to outlast it, but I'm not confident." Is this an example of a promising folk art? Or is it an illustration of the fact that much mass culture tends to be not culture at all, but an opium of the people? ¶ Commenting on the general situation of which this is typical, André Malraux first recognizes the unparalleled extent to which the popular arts have met response from the public until, as he says, the whole of a pulsating, incoherent mass of dreams is the dominant feature of its inward life. Then he adds: "Confronting the great shapeless dream surging out of the unconscious crowds, with its imperious demands, its childish angels and cheap heroes, stand the only forces as powerful as they, and which we acknowledge only by their victory over death." These forces are the forces embodied in the great art of the past with which it is necessary to make connection again if a genuine modern civilization is to be created. "The dialogue between a fantasy life, sweeping over half the world, and the resurrection of a global past is not a minor characteristic of this civilization…culture is the free world's most powerful guardian against the demons of its dreams, its most powerful ally in leading humanity to a dream worthy of man." ¶ Implied in these remarks is the only adequate conception of the role of art or the artist in a technological, or in any other, civilization. But to what extent is what Malraux calls the "dialogue between the shapeless dreams of mass culture and genuine expressions of man's artistic creations" actually taking place? On the one hand, the encouragers of shapeless dreams continue to propagate them, while taking private refuge in their Steinways and their tapestries. On the other, those who should and no doubt would prefer to confront shapeless dreams with genuine products of the creative imagination are, in overwhelming proportion, what it is now fashionable to call "alienated"—from their nation, from the human race, and, often, from the universe itself. Never, with the possible exception of the world of the Roman Empire, has so large a part of the best artistic creation been bitter, despairing, contemptuous, and destructive. With rare exceptions, the works most, and most justly, admired by intellectuals are counsels of despair. We produce parodies, denunciations, and nightmares. On the whole, our best artists are engaged in disrupting patterns, smashing forms, and deliberately cultivating dissonances in painting and music, as well as in poetry, fiction, and drama. They engage in no promising dialogue with either the statesman, the scientist, or the majority of their fellow citizens. They have, in their own way, signed off from their civilization almost as effectively as has the cultivated manufacturer of the shapeless dream. ❡ Commenting on this situation, I wrote a few months ago in *The Saturday Review:* ❡ "Ideally, the business of the 'intellectual'—in the special narrow sense of that word—is to define ultimate values. The business of the statesman, the sociologist, the economist, and the lawmaker is to devise the means by which they can be made to prevail. But rarely have the two groups paid so little attention to one another. The first are still predominately iconoclasts verging toward, if not actually accepting, a nihilistic despair. Many, at least, of the second are full of hopeful plans to abolish racial and economic inequality, to raise still further the standard of living in our own country, to develop the underdeveloped countries, and thus to fulfill the hopes of the world." ❡ Nevertheless, there is precious little meeting of minds in actual dialogue, and because there is not, neither the intellectuals nor their artistic fellows supply what is lacking in even the most benevolent proposal to advance toward a truly humane civilization. ❡ It is certainly not worth while to lecture the artist on his duty to society or to urge him to be optimistic and helpful. He has, indeed, been so admonished from time to time by writers in influential publications of the sort which he dismisses as "middle-brow," but without any result other than an increase in his alienation. Perhaps—as it is actually the central purpose of this whole volume to suggest—the problem of how to promote a rapprochement, to persuade the intellectual and the artist to join rather than to alienate themselves still further from the society which so desperately needs them, might be approached from the opposite direction. Perhaps artists are so completely alienated from the society in which they live partly because it has so persistently alienated itself from them—in one or another of the ways this essay has attempted to describe. If the artist should do something for his society, would it not be advisable for the society to do something more for him than it has done in the past? ❡ Of all human activities, of course, the creation of literature, music, and works of plastic art is most unpredictable, the least responsive to deliberate cultivation. Of all human beings not certified as delinquent or psychopathic, the artist is not infrequently the most stubborn, wayward, suspicious, and rebellious.

The merest suggestion that he can be profitably directed by the nonartist causes his hackles to rise. He wants to be praised and he will usually accept (though often refuses to be grateful for) financial support. But otherwise he wants to be left alone to go his own way. What he believes with considerable justification to be low esteem in which society holds him, he repays with an even lower estimate of those who are not members of his brotherhood. Though he suffers from the fact that he is not sufficiently appreciated, he also glories in it, and (to use the current term) he is of all men the most "inner directed" and, to that extent, anarchistic. ❡ Or so it appears. For society is organized, is aggregated, is interdependent and centrifugal. Its gravitational force is made up of common assumptions, common denominators, commonality. It has ever been intolerant of anarchy, uneasy about the antithetical, fearful of the implied threat to its stability—or even its existence—in contrary thought and action. ❡ And into this category of subtle dangers has fallen —or been pushed—the fierce individualism of the committed artist. For each artist in all times has taken onto himself the severe and exacting burden of independence and singularity which qualifies him to interpret, identify, and symbolize, to view with an unique eye what is, and give form to his vision. It is his ability to do this which makes him an artist as surely as it is a consequence that he shall travel alone an electron's orbit around the nucleus. ❡ Yet his isolation is not estrangement, but a necessary condition to clear sight, like the mountaintop location of the telescope. From this vantage point, with this perspective, he makes his statements about reality in the language or the medium that bespeaks him. ❡ So far so good. Yet if this much is true, it is also true that the artist and society are bound to each other. It is from society that the artist emerges, by society that he is inspired, about society that he must care if there is to be purpose to his effort. Likewise, it is from the artist that society gains its loftier images of itself, gains a sense of the God-given individuality that exists within the whole. ❡ It is a balance fairly struck, although never easily maintained. Society must always guard against its suspicions of differentness, must be willing to grant the exceptional behavior of the artist as the price of receiving from him a comment of value and validity. And the artist must accept the risk that his vision may be flawed, obscure, incomprehensible—which is the price of aspiring to truth. ❡ The only thing neither can risk is alienation from the other.